D0436992

For Ariella, Asher, Olive, Frankie and their classmates – R.R.
For the teachers and pupils of Stepney Primary School, Hull – C.R.

Text copyright © Rachel Rooney 2018
Illustrations copyright © Chris Riddell 2018

First published in Great Britain and in the USA in 2018 by
Otter-Barry Books, Little Orchard, Burley Gate, Herefordshire, HR1 3QS
www.otterbarrybooks.com

All rights reserved

No part of this publication may be reproduced, stored in a retrieval system,
or transmitted, in any form, or by any means, electrical, mechanical,
photocopying, recording or otherwise without the prior written permission
of the publisher or a licence permitting restricted copying. In the United Kingdom
such licences are issued by the Copyright Licensing Agency, Barnard's Inn,
86 Fetter Lane, London EC4A 1EN

A catalogue record for this book is available from the British Library.

ISBN 978-1-91095-987-9

Illustrated with pencil and watercolour

Set in Plantin

Printed in China

9 8 7 6 5 4 3 2 1

Rooney, Rachel,
A kid in my class :
poems /
2018.
33305244257345
ca   12/11/18

KID IN MY
CLASS

Poems by Rachel Rooney

Illustrations by Chris Riddell

Otter-Barry BOOKS

Contents

Dear Reader   9

First   10

Daydreamer   12

Tips for the New Boy   14

The Poet   16

Accident Prone   18

Whizz Kid   20

Joe Bloggs   22

As Shy As   24

Fidget   26

Tomboy   28

Friendship Bench   30

Seeker   32

A Girl   34

Keepy-Uppy Kid   36

Cool   38

Copycat   40

The Crush   42

Joker   44

Don't Walk, Run!   46

Her-Ku	48
Inscrutable	50
Best Friender	52
Ravenous	54
Tough Kid	56
Twins	58
Drama Queen Award	60
Talking Hands	62
Wordsmith	64
Sticker	66
The Artist	68
The Questioner	70
Prefect	72
Dishonest	74
Job Share	76
Substitute Teacher	78
Vacancy	80
The Hamster Speaks	82
About Rachel Rooney	84
About Chris Riddell	85

Dear Reader,

Over time, I have grown fond of everyone that you'll meet here.
I now think of this book as a class full of people rather than
a collection of poems. Of course, in real life we are much more
complicated than they are. We're likely to be a mixture of
several of them – and more besides. I can spot myself in
a number of these characters. How about you?

Rachel Rooney

First

She's there in the playground at eight thirty-two.
The bell rings at nine. She's the first in the queue.
Registration begins. At the top of the list
is her name and the way that she answers, *Here Miss*.

When questions are asked or if one volunteer
is needed, her hand is the first to appear.
Whichever new game is the latest class craze,
she had it first. She'll flaunt it for days.

She's the eldest. First with the party invites,
the badges, the candles, the sparkling tights.
Were she a poem, you'd know where to look:
she'd push her way past to the start of the book.

Daydreamer

His name is called and there's a pause
just long enough to halt a war
tame timber wolves and trim their claws
hide diamonds in a secret drawer
lure dragons to a trick trapdoor
eat pancakes by the Côte d'Azur
discover one last cancer cure
take a penalty and score
– then simply teleport
back to where he was before
sat cross-legged on the floor
to answer with a yawn.

Good Morning.

Tips for the New Boy

The playground is built on top of a graveyard.
Press your ear to the tarmac and you'll hear the undead
scratching on their coffin lids.

Once, we caught the school cook sneezing
into the tomato sauce as she was stirring it.
Never choose the pizza option.

There's a two-way mirror in the girls' changing room
(the one next to ours).

Our teacher has a morbid fear of frogs. Don't mention them.
Always clear your throat before entering the classroom.

We're allowed to draw on the cover of our learning journal.

The lock in the boys' toilet always gets stuck.
Best to leave the door slightly open.

When the fire alarm is tested,
the first person out of the class wins a prize.

Each summer, one classmate is kept back for a whole year.
It's usually the teacher's favourite pupil.

The headmaster doesn't like you to knock on his door
when you're delivering a message.
He prefers you to sing it through the keyhole.

On Fridays, we always bring in a box of Gummy Bears
to share with our friends.

Don't believe everything you've been told.
Only one of these statements is true.

The Poet

The light through the blind is a poem,
the way it illuminates air.
And the shadows that fall
on the floor and the wall
are signs that a poem is there.

The tick of the clock is a poem,
even the spaces between.
The echo of heels
and corridor squeals
are proof that a poem has been.

An empty white page is a poem,
a place where the magic occurs.
It's a home from a home
where ideas can roam.
At least for the poet, hers.

Accident Prone

Poked a pencil in his eye.
Swallowed a bluebottle fly.
Split his trousers in PE.
Accidentally.

Dropped his lunchbox in the mud.
Left the taps on; caused a flood.
Snapped his glasses into three.
Accidentally.

Tore the brand new wall display.
Let our hamster out to play.
Broke the teacher's DVD.
Accidentally.

Styled his hair with paint and glue.
Locked himself inside the loo.
Tripped his laces, scraped his knee.
Accidentally.

Trapped his fingers in the door.
Twice the size they were before.
Taken off to A&E.
Very carefully.

Whizz Kid

Question 1)

I get 3 Maths questions right, she gets 30 Maths questions right.
How many more questions does she answer correctly?

Answer: *Loads.*

Question 2)

She answers 12 Maths questions in 2 minutes.
What is the average number of seconds spent on each question?

Answer: *Not very long.*

Question 3)

The teacher gives us 1 merit for every 5 Maths questions
we answer correctly. She has 6 merits.
How many questions did she get right?

Answer: *More than me.*

Question 4)

Her homework is in her school bag, which is 5 metres from the teacher's desk. My homework is on my kitchen table which is 3,355 metres from the teacher's desk.

How much further away is my homework than hers?

Answer: *Miles.*

Question 5)

She has come top in every Maths test this year. What are the chances I'll beat her next time?

Answer: *One in a squillion.*

Joe Bloggs

See that person over there,
the average child with mousy hair?
The boy who's neither tall nor short.
Not thin or fat. A so-so sort.

The type of lad who isn't last
or first in tests. Not slow. Not fast.
A child who's neither nerd nor joker.
Just average and mediocre.

His face is OK, I suppose.
He has two eyes, a mouth, a nose.
He's been with us since last September.
What's his name? I can't remember.

As Shy As

a crocus in February
the nose of a mole
a new moon's smile
an everlasting gobstopper
the curl of a fern
a penny wedged in a slot
crushed lavender
a red letterbox
a simile that wants to be a metaphor.
That shy.

Fidget

Nose fiddler. Desk drummer.
Tune hummer. Pencil twiddler.

Face maker. Chair tipper.
Hair snipper. Ruler breaker.

Knuckle clicker. Hole puncher.
Toe scruncher. Nit picker.

Seat shifter. Page scribbler.
Lip nibbler. Thought drifter.

Tomboy

Not glitter and glitz. Not hair clips and bangles,
painting of toenails and doodled lovehearts.

More baseball cap worn at a jaunty right-angle,
skateboard and shin pads, arm-wrestling, darts.

Not twirling pink tutus and crushes on singers,
pouts in the mirror for selfies, fake fur.

More spit on the sidelines, whistle through fingers.
Not a Tom. Not a boy. Just being more her.

Friendship Bench

There's a kid in our class – her name's not called at register.
It's carved into brass and nailed to the bench we bought for her.

My fingertips trace that absent name. *In Memory…*
I can picture her face. Perhaps she still remembers me?

31

Seeker

Eyes as wide as continents brim with the water between.
Seeks a different future. Looks back on what has been.

Mouth seeks another language. Shapes a different air.
Unfamiliar classroom words. The other, whispered prayer.

Heart seeks home. One it left and one it took along.
Echoes in the distance. Skips to a playground song.

A Girl

A girl in our class has a faraway look.
Head in the clouds. Nose in a book.
Tiptoes around. The soles of her feet
are raw from the playground's heat.

A girl in our class has an expert eye.
Views the world in black and white.
Open and shut. Her wide eyes blink.
Sharpens her pencil. Thinks.

A girl in our class has pale, thin skin.
Bones of a bird. Heart on a string.
She's over there, in the shade of a tree.
Won't come down until three.

Keepy~Uppy Kid

He's the Keepy-Uppy Kid.
He's the best the school has seen.
Can he keep it off the floor
and increase his score?   Sixteen.

Watch the Keepy-Uppy Kid.
Let him prove his skills to you.
Can his feet stay undefeated
without cheating?   Thirty two.

Hail the Keepy-Uppy Kid.
He's the champion of us all.
Can he show he's extra nifty
and reach fifty?   Drops the ball.

Cool

As cool as a cucumber?
No. He's way cooler than that.
Cooler than frozen peas, vanilla brain freeze,
numb blue toes and ice cubes stuck to the tongue.
He thinks he's minus thirty degrees.

He thinks he's a sub-zero hero. A dude.
A geezer who's too cool for school uniform.
Chews on mint gum.
Calls me *Swot, Loser, Dumb*.
Tells me to chill. Thinks he is it.

Well, he's not.

Copycat

You think it's funny, don't you?

                            You think it's funny, don't you?

But it's really, really annoying.

                            But it's really, really annoying.

Oh shut up and go away.

                            Oh shut up and go away.

If you don't stop, I'm telling.

                            If you don't stop, I'm telling.

OK, then…

                            OK, then…

Subdermatoglyphic.

                            Sub-dermato-glyphic.

Err... Antidisestablishmentarianism.

Err... Anti-dis-establishment-arian-ism.

Hmm...hippopotomonstrosesquippedaliophobia.

Hmm... Hippo-poto-monstro-sesquip-pedalio-phobia.

How about Pneumonoultramicroscopicsilicovolcanoconiosis?

How about Pneumo-noultra-micro-scopic-silico-volcano-coniosis?

Aha! I've got it!

Aha! I've got it!

I'm a stupid copycat with nothing else better to do...

The Crush

I haven't got a crush. He's just a boy.
I swear he's just a boy who is my friend.
This rumour is beginning to annoy.
Your idle gossip really needs to end.

The way his top lip curls before he breaks
into a smile, the way he rakes his hair,
the quick and clever jokes he quietly makes:
these little things are neither here nor there.

The way his eyes light up electric blue
whenever he explains some new idea,
the way he keeps my place within the queue
means *zilch* to me. Am I being clear?

For all those reasons given (see above),
I'm not in love. Repeat. I'm not in love.

Joker

The boy next to me is a bore.
All the jokes that he tells, I ignore.
His timing is wrong
and the punchlines are long,
rather weak and on the whole, highly predictable.

Don't Walk, Run!

His legs don't walk so he wheels himself around in a chair.

When people ask why, he says he had a fight with a very grizzly bear.

Or, fell a full five miles from the top of Everest.

Or, he's saving them for best.

Or, he's resting up in preparation for his astronaut training.

Or, their batteries need replacing.

Or, he simply overheated in the Gobi desert sun.

Or, they've turned to plum jelly.

Or, they're stuck to the seat with super-glue.

Or, they were swapped with an octopus who had two to spare.

His legs don't walk so he wheels in a chair instead.

And he runs in his head.

Her~ku

Me Me Me Me Me
Me Me Me Me Me Me Me
Me Me Me Me Me

Inscrutable

What goes on inside your head
you do not speak about, and so
I think I'll make it up instead.

You're like a book that must be read.
But I can't read you. I don't know
what goes on inside your head.

Will you speak? Is language dead?
I'd really like the answer. Though
I think I'll make it up instead.

Your silent stare makes me see red.
But unlike me, you never show
what goes on inside your head.

Did you hear what I just said?
It might be *Yes*. It might be *No*.
I think I'll make it up instead.

You'll take your secrets to your bed
but I will give it one last go...
What goes on inside your head?

I think I'll make it up instead.

Best Friender

She'll be your best friend if...
you take her side in the argument
you don't tell Miss that she cheated
you whisper to her the name of the person you secretly love
you vote for her to be Team Captain
you give her the first turn on your phone
you share your lunchbox crisps with her
you save her a space on the bench
you'll be her best friend.

Too late.
She's got a new best friend now.

Ravenous

He cannot wait much longer for his lunch. Until it comes
he'll excavate his nostril for a morsel or some crumbs,
then peel himself a crusty scab that's baked upon his thumb.

He starts to chew his fingernails while standing in the queue.
He could murder a beefburger or, of course, a horse or two.
(And most exotic creatures you'd encounter in a zoo.)

He's gnawing on his fingers now – but not the fishy kind.
He rumbles like Vesuvius in AD 79.
If someone doesn't feed him soon, I'm sure he'll lose his mind.

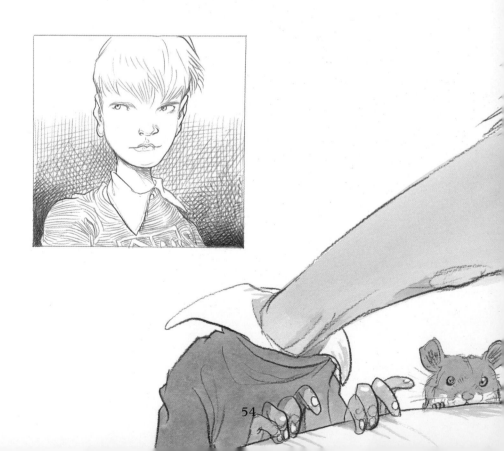

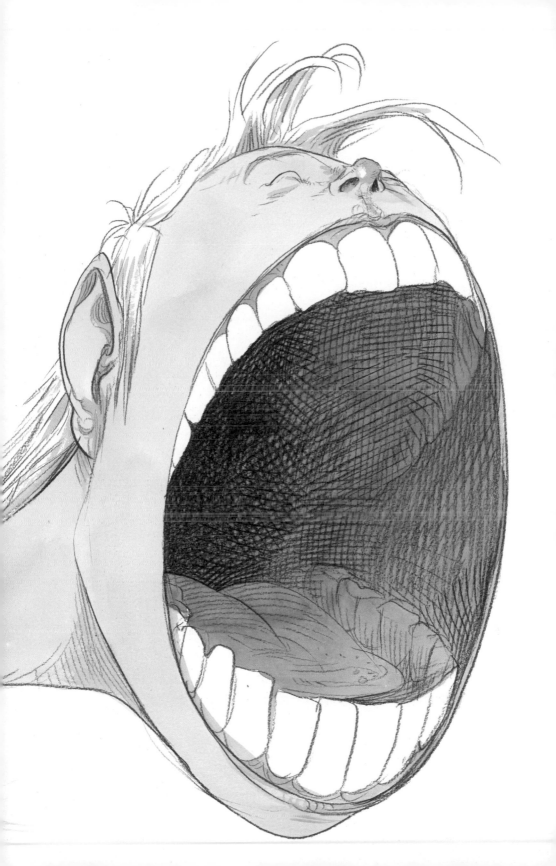

Tough Kid

It's tough being him.
Everything's boring. Sad.
Things drive him mad.
And when they do – Watch Out!
You're sure to get it.
Oi...Ow...Ouch...
You did? Too bad.
He's not scared of nothing.
Nobody. Never. Nah.
Which means that he is.
Tough kid. Not tough enough.

I know – I once met his dad.

Twins

One has hazel eyes. Her auburn hair
is parted into plaits and tied with bows.
Freckles spread across her cheeks and nose
as if some butterfly had landed there.

From her coat, two gloves swing on a thread.
Both shoelaces sport a double knot.
She wears shades at break-time when it's hot
and if it's not, wears warm ear-muffs instead.

Always wins the school three-legged race,
loves Siamese cats and sucking candy twist,
bends her thumb right back to touch her wrist
and recently was fitted with a brace.

The other is identical. The same
but has a pinkish scar, another name.

Drama Queen Award

Missing Rubber
Scraped Knee
Best Friend Fallout 3
Squashed Banana
Cold Sore
Foot Caught in the Door
Uninvited
Broken Nail
Packed Lunch Gone Stale
Boy Trouble
Not True
Lost My Place in the Queue
Voted Out
Wasn't Me
Sheep in the Nativity

(Applause)

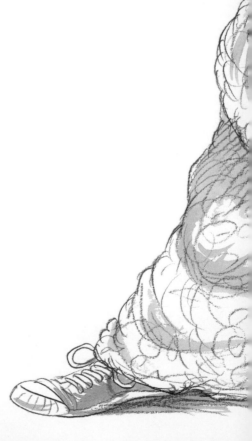

Talking Hands

She raises up her open thumb and forefinger
as if measuring a gap of air.
I say: *Word*

Fingers outstretched with palms facing, she rotates her hands
in opposite directions,
as if she were polishing both sides of a two-way mirror.
I say: *Sign*

She cups her hand to her ear
as if holding an empty sea shell against it.
I say: *Listen*

Her two V-shaped fingers are held to her eyes, then turn
and move towards me
as if they were inquisitive antennae.
I say: *Look*

We shake hands with ourselves: *Friends*

Wordsmith

He is a walking dictionary:
the stuff of fact and fiction.
He's a child who's even speedier
than googling Wikipedia.
He'll offer no apology
for roaming terminology
and clearly likes to demonstrate
his lexicon is ambulate.

Occasionally he'll bore us,
but he makes a great Thesaurus.

Sticker

If he sits still on his cushion
and can line up without pushing
or he doesn't make a mess when doing art,
if he says he's sorry or he
doesn't interrupt the story
then he gets a shiny sticker on his chart.

If he passes out the pens
and says thank-you to his friends
or recites his one-times-table off by heart,
if he wears his coat at play
and he doesn't swear all day
then he gets a second sticker on his chart.

If he eats up all his lunch
or remembers not to punch
then our teacher says he's choosing to be smart.
And although I don't agree,
he can watch a DVD
now he's got three shiny stickers on his chart.

The Artist

The artist doodles oodles of poodles.
He pens a red wren on his left hand,
gives it wings for fingers.
He chalks stick insects onto brick,
and defaces the ladies in newspapers
with moustaches and glasses.

The artist coins eyeballs and footballs into walls,
inks an arrow between his skinny ribs with a thin-nib felt-tip
and shapes a yeti from spaghetti.
He tattoos a black and blue rose round a bruise,
squiggles a squid in dribble,
muddies the puddles for fun.

The Questioner

No, you won't work with a partner.
Yes, please write it out in best.
No, you can't draw in the margin.
Yes, this is an actual test.
No, you're not allowed a rubber.
Yes, do put your name and date.
No, you can't go to the toilet.
Yes, I think that it can wait.
No, it doesn't feel like fever.
Yes, I'd take your jumper off.
No, I haven't got a cough drop.
Yes, that's quite a nasty cough.
No, the spider isn't deadly.
Yes, I've trapped it in a cup.
No, you can't discuss the answers.
Yes, you have to finish up.
No, I'm sure the clock is working.
Yes, it's true that time can fly.
No, you can't complete it later.
Yes, that is the bell.
Goodbye.

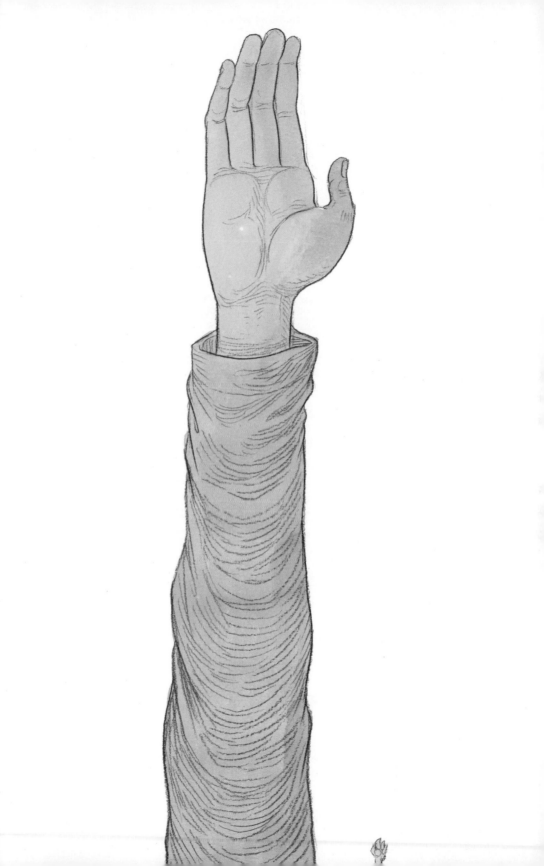

Prefect

Perfectly kind. Perfectly good.
Perfect does what perfect should.
Perfect white teeth, perfectly straight.
Perfect parents at the gate.
Perfectly balanced. Perfectly dressed.
Perfect score in the Prefect Test.
Perfect brain in a perfect skull.

Perfectly nice but perfectly dull.

Dishonest

He swears on his mother's life he wasn't there.
And if he was there
he swears on his mother's life it wasn't him.
And if it was him
he swears on his mother's life it was an accident.
And if it wasn't an accident
he swears on his mother's life someone egged him on.
And if they didn't egg him on
he swears on his mother's life that he didn't start it.

And when she meets him at the school gates
she'll always believe him.
God's Honest Truth.

Job Share

Mondays and Tuesdays are glum days and rule days.
I think I'm too ill to be going to school days.

Got it all wrong days. Rotten and long days.
Days when I feel like I'm failing some test.

MR. ROTE

I prefer Wednesdays, Thursdays, Fridays.
Laughter and smile days. Better by miles days.

I'm on my way days. Work, rest and play days.
Give it a try and you might be surprised days.

Soar in the sky days. Bursting with pride days.
Being alive days. Those days are best.

MISS MUSE

Substitute Teacher

Whatshisname came in.
He found his way about.
Then when he found the door,
Whatshisname went out.

Vacancy

(For Jessica Rooney)

Our Teaching Assistant is leaving today.
She says she's too old to be bending her knees
or wiping the noses that run in our families.
What can we give her?
A hankie embroidered with pink, silk roses.
A walking stick.
And three big sneezes.
Achoo!
Achoo!
Achoo!

Our Teaching Assistant is leaving today.
She's tired and retiring but says she will miss
all our cheek, our stories, the secrets we whisper.
What shall we give her?
A pen that won't leak.
The clean, white sheets of a writing book.
And three blown kisses.
Mwah!
Mwah!
Mwah!

Our Teaching Assistant is leaving today.
She says that she's been here for thirty-five years
and yes, it is sad but they're happy tears.
What do we give her?
This poem we wrote in a card that we made.
A chocolate medal.
And three loud cheers for our T.A.
Hip Hip Hooray!
Hip Hip Hooray!
Hip Hip Hooray!

The Hamster Speaks

I missed out on the school trip but I am an ace historian.
I've studied Greeks and Romans, Tudors and the odd Victorian.
My knowledge of geography is really quite superior,
from deserts of Death Valley to the ice lakes of Siberia.

I'm good at Maths – I can convert a fraction to a decimal.
My long division is superb, my geometry professional.
I've studied water cycles, butterflies and reproduction,
all the properties of solids, liquids, gas. And heat conduction.

I punctuate my sentences: they're complex and grammatical.
And spelling words like xylophone is seldom problematical.
My ears can pick out pitch and tempo, rhythm and percussion,
and I know Kandinsky painted abstract art and that he's Russian.

I've learned about religion from Baha'i to Christianity
and now I'm learning French. I wonder how I've kept my sanity.
Perhaps that's why I chew on bars instead of vegetation,
and I exercise my muscles with repeated wheel rotation.

I'll take a nap while others write up in their learning journal.
Maybe, like me, they should consider being more nocturnal?

RACHEL ROONEY trained and worked as a
special needs teacher while bringing up her three sons.
Now one of the UK's most highly acclaimed poets,
she visits schools, leads poetry workshops
and performs at festivals, including the national
touring festival The Children's Bookshow.
Her first poetry collection, *The Language of Cat*,
won the CLPE Prize (CLiPPA) in 2012.
Her second collection, *My Life as a Goldfish*,
was shortlisted for the CLiPPA in 2015.
She has been a judge for the Betjeman poetry prize
and chair of judges for the CLiPPA in 2017.
She is also a National Poetry Day ambassador.
Rachel Rooney lives in Brighton.

CHRIS RIDDELL has won many illustration awards for
his work, including the UNESCO Prize,
the Kate Greenaway Medal (on three occasions)
and the Hay Festival Medal for Illustration.
His books include the *Ottoline* titles, the *Goth Girl* series,
the first book of which won the Costa Children's Book
Award, the New York Times best-selling series,
The Edge Chronicles, with Paul Stewart and
The Sleeper and The Spindle with Neil Gaiman.
Chris was the Waterstones Children's Laureate UK
2015-2017 and was appointed Book Trust's first official
ambassador in 2017. He is president of the School Library
Association and currently artist in
residence for the National Youth Orchestra.
He lives and works in Brighton.